Love
Yourself First

Dedication for those that we remember:

To the millions of Jews and others that died in the Holocaust.

Dedication for those in the present:

To the millions that work tirelessly to make our lives better and are often not noticed in our busy world.

Love Yourself First

CAT

Order this book online at www.trafford.com
or email orders@trafford.com

Most Trafford titles are also available at major online book retailers.

Printed in the United States of America.

ISBN: 978-1-4269-5807-6 (sc)
ISBN: 978-1-4269-5806-9 (e)

Trafford rev. 12/09/2011

 www.trafford.com

North America & international
toll-free: 1 888 232 4444 (USA & Canada)
phone: 250 383 6864 ♦ fax: 812 355 4082

Love Yourself First
Contents

Chapter 1

My Granddaughter Arrives

It all began on a day filled to the brim with activity and emotion. A day overfilled with love and sorrow all at the same time. A day almost too heavy to carry on my back. It was a day that was waited for, a day that was hoped for, a day that a new life would begin. My daughter was about to give birth to her third child. She was at the tender age of twenty three and already carried a heavy load. The birth of a child should have been a happy day, but it also came with so many other emotions.

My daughter was not married and she already had two children from two different men. Unfortunately those men showed no interest in the sons they helped create. They did contribute something though. They passed on life that formed into two wonderful boys, my two grandsons. I won't go into all of those details now, for it would take us away from the special event of the day. It would take us away from the beautiful moment that was about to magically materialize. My daughter was about to give birth and all my attention was focused on this new soul entering the world. The special event occurred on May the eleventh, 2007. My daughter gave birth to her first daughter, my first granddaughter. This little being came into this world with her first cry. A sound of life exploded as oxygen filled her tiny lungs, and she cried. Life arrived and it was a blessing.

My daughter, Alice, went into premature labor a few times before this day in May, but fortunately the doctors and the powers above kept the fetus inside my daughter. The fetus needed a little more time for growth and lung maturity. My granddaughter who was born six weeks premature, despite all odds, came out perfectly healthy. She was small but strong and tipped the scale at five pounds one ounce.

That special day came in May when I was at work. Alice, my daughter, called me that day to tell me she was in labor. I was determined that I would be there. I was only twenty miles away in a different hospital working as a nurse. Yes, I am a nurse and have been working as one since the age of twenty-one. I could not just up and leave my position at work to go to where my daughter was. Nurses cannot just leave a job with a simple phone call. I needed to find my own relief. I called other nurses that were not working that day and asked if they would come in to work for me. Fortunately, someone who was out having lunch with a friend agreed to come in when they were done eating. I wanted to accomplish as much as possible so my replacement wouldn't have to work hard. I was grateful that she was coming in to work for me and that was my way of showing gratitude. After the other nurse arrived I drove home to quickly change out of my work clothes and put on my regular dumpy comfy clothes. I arrived at the hospital a bit rushed but glad to be there. No time to think about myself, I was there for my daughter. I was there for the start of a new precious life.

I entered the hospital and with a few twists, turns, and lifts from an elevator I found the room where my daughter was located. She was in bed and already was dressed in a nondescript hospital gown. She laid there hooked up to a monitor. An IV found its home in a vein in her forearm. She looked tired and a bit uncomfortable, but she was still able to engage in conversation. I equated that with being in the beginning stages of labor and took in a deep breath for I could slow down a bit and catch my breath.

In her room there were many other people. The room was actually a bit crowded with a variety of different folks. In a soft relaxing chair next to Alice's bed was a very large set woman. I'd say she was in her late forties and would have estimated that she was about three times my size. She was an acquaintance of my daughter. Another person in this crowded room was a man that was once married to my daughter. Yes, Alice had been married for a few brief moments in her life. Their marriage didn't even last a year, but there were questionable thoughts that Alice's baby might also be his. Due to the uncertainty he stuck around for the big event. His mother was also there and she was acting kind even though she might or might not be the grandmother to the child that was coming into this world. Oh, and I can't forget that my first ex-husband and his wife were in and out of the room too. My ex-husband was remarried to a woman that had two kids from two different men. Sounds like a familiar story, doesn't it? Despite the various backgrounds of everyone there, we all got along on this particular day for we were all there for one reason. We were there for the birth of a new life.

Alice's labor progressed and the contractions became harder and more frequent. The light and the noise in the room were starting to bother her, so the lights were turned off and people slowly sauntered out of the room. I quietly remained with her. With all her hard work of having one contraction after another the cervix was not cooperating. It did not want to dilate. Every time the nurse or the doctor would check her cervix I quietly hoped that the diameter would get larger. It seemed like things were actually getting worse than better. The cervix was actually becoming thicker and not dilating. The plan of having a normal vaginal delivery was becoming more distant as the minutes and the hours passed. The doctor then started talking about doing a cesarian section. Alice, at first, was upset about the idea. It took some time for her to ponder over this new idea. Her other two children were born by natural vaginal deliveries and she just assumed that this one would be too. In the end Alice realized that this was something she had to accept and she needed to move forward for her unborn child's sake. She signed the consent to go ahead with the C-Section.

The room in which the cesarean section would be taking place in was being prepared. The doctor and the nurses were getting prepared and dressed for the part. Alice was allowed to have one family member in the room with her. I was not going to persuade her to take me. I wanted her to make her own decision. She needed to decide on her own who she felt should be in there. Should the man that was possibly the father of the infant be in the room with her? What if it wasn't his kid? In the end she picked me and I rushed into hospital attire. I wore a long sleeved yellow gown that hung about a foot from the floor.

I stood right by my daughter's head and concentrated on how she was doing. A barrier of sheets were draped close to her head, so that she would not see the knife when it sliced into her abdomen. There was a lot of activity happening on the other side of the sheets. I did see moments of the procedure when I briefly peered over the barrier of the sheets. One thing that stood out in my mind was when I saw her fallopian tubes coming out to be cut. That had been a prearranged plan for her to be made sterile. She had held many uncertainties about this procedure but did sign the consent before coming into the operating room. I also saw the magic of the day, I saw the baby being taken out of my daughter's abdomen. I witnessed what was done by the doctor's hands. His gloved hands were so practiced in this maneuver that it seemed like he was a magician magically taking a rabbit out of a hat.

Once the baby was out I quietly went into my silent high gear to watch every move and feeling around me. If there were any rushed movements or serious looks on their faces I would have become concerned. As I observed the scene everyone seemed relaxed and I even heard them have a little giggle. The staff was talking with each other, as calm as cumbers, as if they were just sitting out on their patio having a barbeque. I knew then that everything was going good. I took in a deep breath, relaxed, and spoke with my daughter. We talked about how beautiful her new daughter was.

The baby was taken to the nursery and Alice was taken to an area for supervision. Everybody that had been in Alice's hospital room before the procedure had now journeyed over to the nursery. It was a happy and exciting moment in that well traveled, narrow hallway of the hospital. All the people that had been in Alice's room were now standing in this hallway looking through the glass walls into the nursery. Relief and happy talk surrounded the area. We all remarked how cute the new baby looked.

I started talking with the "might be" father and his mother. They were talking about the baby and how she looked like the man that had once been Alice's husband. At this point, the father of this baby was not medically determined. DNA testing would need to be done to come up with the definitive answer. Inwardly I wondered but kept such thoughts to myself. I wanted to keep this day a happy day, a positive day.

While I was conversing with them I started to feel extremely dizzy and woozy. It became difficult for me just to stand in the hallway near the nursery. My legs were wobbly and weak. I politely decided to tell them that I was going back to the room. I figured that I could walk to the room that was going to be Alice's hospital room. Conversation had become a huge job for me and I thought that I just needed to relax.

Before I continue I would like to share something with you. First off, I must first tell you that I am not an alcoholic. I might drink a few sips of wine every few years but that is all. I share this information with you now, so you can understand that the following behavior was not alcohol related. Anyway as I headed back to my daughter's room my legs became weak and awkward. It might have looked like I was a sloppy drunk to any stranger passing by. Each and every step made me feel uncoordinated and off balance. Movements were almost out of my control. I was walking like a drunken sailor. Visually, things also went haywire. The floor was no longer the floor and the walls were no longer walls. With some luck I somehow managed to get to my daughter's room.

I started inwardly blaming myself for not eating or drinking for the past twelve hours. Inwardly I scolded myself. I should have had something to drink. What was the matter with me? Maybe I just needed to drink. I forced myself to drink the water from the plastic water pitcher sitting on the table by the hospital bed. I swallowed large hard gulps of water while still being mad at myself inwardly. I knew about dehydration so I was at fault, "Come on Cat..... you should have taken something to drink! You Fool!" I was silently and inwardly scolding myself. I felt responsible for feeling dizzy and mad at myself at the same time. After all I am a nurse and I should have known better. After drinking the water I looked around in the hospital room where I was sitting. I saw that there was a private bathroom about thirty feet from where I was located. During my scanning of the room I soon discovered that I was not alone in that room. The heavy lady that had been in the other room was now here parked in a lounge chair. She saw me and noticed that I was not looking too healthy around the gills.

Without any words said, I staggered over to the bathroom and sat on the toilet. Things eventually began to affect my stomach, and I went from sitting on the throne to kneeling right in front of it. I was dizzy and holding on to the porcelain for dear life. I started with projectile vomiting. What I mean by that was that the vomit just erupted like a volcano and came out of my mouth and nose with an angry eruption. It must have been heard by the heavy lady in the room for soon I was not alone. Now, at that point I am not sure who said what to whom but two nurses had arrived in the room with a wheelchair accompanying them. I had looked at them and they were just floating in front of me. It made me nauseated just to look at things directly. I clutched even tighter to my round stabilizer. At that point the toilet was my close and trusted companion.

The nurses started to ask me questions in between my dry and productive heaves. They wanted to take me down to the emergency department to get checked out. In between dizziness and reverse contractions of my stomach, I tried to explain to them that I was not feeling well because I had not eaten or had anything to drink for many hours. In my words I had tried to tell them that I was really alright just a little dehydrated. They continued to question me and I continued to see them swirl around in space right in front of my eyes. Finally, with reluctance, I climbed into the wheelchair half bent over as if I was a crippled person. I had the appearance of a ghost since I was so pale. Somehow via the wheels on a chair and the mechanical skills of the elevator, I swiftly arrived in the hospital's emergency department.

Time of Reflection

I believe that all things happen for a reason. Why and when they happen is still a mystery to me, but they do happen. Why did I get sick on the day my daughter gave birth to her daurghter? Why was it so difficult for me to walk back to my daughter's hospital room? Why was my daughter's friend sitting there as I tried to gulp down water? If she wasn't there I probably wouldn't have gotten the help that I needed. I now see that it was just a piece of a puzzle fitting together. I now see that it was a blessing that it all happened the way it did. I was right there in the hospital and was taken into their care even though it was the furthest thing from my mind. It does seem strange that things happen to all of us when we least expect them. They happen for a reason, often for a good reason. Today, years later, I am grateful for the sequence of events that happened that day.

Chapter II

My Health History

Why did I get so dizzy and nauseated the day my grandaughter was born? I had thought that I was just dehydrated. I knew that I did not drink or eat for most of the day. I figured that I needed to look further back into my health history. That seemed like a logical thing to do so my mind flickered over some of my old physical history. One thing that I could count on was the fact that in the past all of my physical troubles were fixable.

One very memorable problem had been extremely painful menstral cycles. They would get worse after every child that I bore, and I had three healthy children which is one very positive thing in my life. The problem was that I was growing a huge fibroid in my uterus and had endometriosis throughout. In other words I had tissue growing freely inside and outside of my uterus where it did not belong. I would stop living a normal life for a few days every month. I would count out the days on the calendar and know when my period was coming and then I would make sure that I didn't have any activity planned during that time. The pain would get so intense that at times I would curl up into a ball and hold a boiling hot water bottle to my pelvic area. I took medication every month for this problem but the medications soon ate their way through the wall of my stomach. My stomach wall could not continue to handle the medications. In time I started bleeding within my intestinal tract. The bleeding dropped my hemoglobin down to the number six which required me to receive a blood transfusion.

I lived with this problem for way too many years. I wasn't a squeaky wheel so the problem was handled very lightly. All of the male doctors, *notice I said male*, would prescribe medications and send me on my way. I understand that one has to experience something to have a true appreciation for the experience. I forgive the many male doctors because they never had gruelingly painful periods. They were simply men. Luckily, I found a physician that diagnosed the problem with the snap of his fingers and said that he would schedule surgery for me with a blink of an eye. With my fibroids being so big he said that my body tried to go into labor every month to get rid of its insides. He had clearly seen all of the haywire and mess growing inside my body. I didn't need to suffer every month like I had done for years. I simply needed a common female surgery. I went for the surgery, which was a partial hysterectomy. It put an end to all of the suffering that had happened monthly like clockwork.

My next physical ailment was kidney stones. The pain associated with those stones was so intense it had me rolling around on the floor. That was a fixable problem too. The stones were broken up by lithotripsy which put an end to that problem. I was grateful that in life some things are so easy to fix.

I had some other minor physical conditions, but they are very easy to live with. I have osteoporosis and hyperlipidemia. In others words my bones are missing some cells which make them too hollow and my blood was too rich in fat. As a kid I had your normal childhood illnesses like chicken pox and once I had broken a bone in my leg but nothing big. Physically everything else worked pretty good in my book, so what was all that nausea and vomiting about on May the eleventh of 2007, the day my granddaughter came into the world?

Time of Reflection

To all of my friends out there, I beg you to let your voice be heard. If I had spoken out in an entirely different way I might have gotten the help I needed sooner. I might not have had to suffer intense monthly menstral pain for so many years. I might have been able to get help earlier on. The whole experience taught me that being the quiet polite patient is not often the right thing to do. I needed to speak up for myself. I needed to make others stop and listen to what I had to say.

If you feel you are not being heard, try a different approach or try talking to someone else that might listen. Not all people are good listeners and they often give ginger coated answers. We need to take the responsibility and get the answers we are looking for. Don't settle until your soul feels satisfied.

Chapter III

What Went Wrong?

What went wrong on that day that my granddaughter was brought into this world? Why did something so wonderful as a birth of healthy child turn into a trying day? Well, let me share that with you.

After finally agreeing to get into the wheelchair from my toilet savior, I arrived in the E.R. at their registration desk. I had trouble communicating and answering simple questions since I had felt so sick. I was sitting hunched over in the wheelchair fighting the feeling of the world spinning around me. After our unsuccessful conversation, the annoyed receptionist typed up the papers that were needed for the next step of my treatment. I was wheeled over to the next area and taken into a room. With some assistance I dressed into the hospital attire. Next an intervenous line became nestled into a vein in my arm. Fluids then poured into my blood stream which I probably needed at that time. Another pick to my arm was done to remove blood for testing.

After sometime I was wheeled out on my stretcher to the X-ray department. It really didn't make much sense to me what all the tests were about. No one explained what they were doing to me or why they were doing it. I was just a person on a stretcher. I was just a number on a page in a book. After I had the test in the CAT scan department I noticed something, something that briefly rattled my soul. The lady that did the CAT scan was so kind to me after the procedure that it left some questions in my gut. That strange gut feeling only lasted a brief moment before I felt my normal defenses kick back into place.

After my CAT scan I was just lying alone in a room with my only companion, the intravenous fluids. They were studiously doing their job of feeding me fluids. Finally after some time had passed the emergency room physician sauntered into my room to talk to me. This short man looked down at the paperwork in my chart and then looked directly up at me. He didn't seem to have much time on his side so he didn't waste anytime with small talk. He told me straight out that I had a …..brain tumor. "I have… WHAT?" I asked. I knew what he said but it was a tough thing to register so quickly. Did he mean me? Why would I have a brain tumor? This was too raw a thought. "Yes," he flatly said, "you have a brain tumor." I began to start thinking rapidly and many things swirled around through my mind. Time seemed to have stopped briefly while I tried to digest the news. Why did I have a tumor? I thought I was just dehydrated.

This was supposed to be a special day, the birth of a baby girl. Why was this happening to me? Why was it happening on that particular day? What did I do to deserve this? Please, just tell me why……

I was left alone for the doctor and the nurse had their jobs to do in the emergency room. I was left there completely alone. I was

13

on the stretcher with the intravenous fluids. At that point the IV fluids were the only constant thing holding the minutes together. Funny how much the day had changed. I had been at work, driven to this hospital, been in a crowded room in the maternity ward, saw my granddaughter being born, to being completely alone in the emergency room. All in a day's work I saw the birth of my granddaughter to being diagnosis with a brain tumor. It all happened within a few short hours of each other. I was too confused to know how to feel. Should I be mad that I had such a horrible diagnosis or should I be glad that they found it while I was under the roof of a hospital?

The next step that was taken was to transfer me via an ambulance to a larger hospital facility, a place that had neurosurgeons and neurologists aboard their ship. I needed to be in a facility that was capable of taking care of someone with a brain tumor. It was a very jolty ride lying on the stretcher in the back of an ambulance. I had never been in a moving vehicle lying flat and looking out backwards. It took all of my concentration to not feel nauseated. Each turn felt like I would fall off the narrow stretcher I was strapped onto.

We somehow arrived in one piece at this larger hospital. I was placed in a room behind many curtains. I was now in this other hospital's ER. Again I was by myself, lying on a stretcher not knowing my future. I was alone in a busy ER with other sick patients near me. I was no longer thinking about my nausea in a moving vehicle. Other thoughts started to occupy my head and I started to check out the area I was located in.

My eyes scanned the area and I looked at the designs in the curtains hanging near my bed. Now, my thinking process had time to start seeing things more clearly. All things around me became clearer and clearer. The clearer things became, the sharper I felt them. I started with the salt water streaming down from my eyes as the thoughts of death swirled around in my head.

Through all of this turmoil someone finally did come into my room behind all of the curtains. A wonderful nurse came to comfort me and that was a huge help. I voiced my fears straight to her. I held nothing back. After all, sitting alone with a horrible diagnosis was no easy task. She felt that I needed to see the doctor and she went to make that happen.

In a short while an elderly doctor with thinning white hair, who had probably seen his fill of life and death, approached me. His upper extremities trembled and in my mind I had already diagnosed him with Parkinson's. My attention was totally focused on him, I no longer saw the patterns in the curtains surrounding my bed. Following behind him was an intern but I could not concentrate on him at that moment.

Basic introductions took place. I was impatient for all I wanted was for him to answer one question for me. I looked at him straight in his eyes and asked, "Do I have cancer?" He looked totally serious back at me and for a brief moment our souls were communicating with each other. He started to talk slowly and with a monotone voice stated, "It's probably benign." That means it is not *cancer.* Yes, hooray it was not those nasty cells reeking havoc in my brain! I took his hand and thanked him and the powers from up above for that wonderful news. He finally did have a smile break onto his deeply lined face of experience. I thanked him at least six times. Almost too many times to the point that it could have caused a nuisance. My concentration on the curtains had long ago vanished after this marvelous revelation. Who needed curtains at a time like this? Who cared that I was alone on this hospital stretcher? Who cared that the tumor laid heavily in a high traffic area of my brain? Who cared that the future was unknown? Who cared that life had a way of leading us up and down many paths of life? I was ready to face the world. I was on a journey and I could only move forward.

CAT

Time of Reflection

I look back at those times and realize that we all need the courage to stand alone. I had to be alone with my diagnosis. The only thing close to me at the time was my intravenous fluid. To me, being alone was something totally scary. But at those moments I needed to believe and trust in myself. I needed the strength to handle my own problems. Lying alone on the hospital stretcher was a time that I needed to pull in all of my own energy and strength. The first and formost thing that I needed was to trust and love myself.

I know that many of us out there are thrust into many trying and difficult moments, but during those times, believe in yourself. If a girlfriend left you and went back with an old boyfriend, love yourself first. If the kids at school bullied you because you are homosexual, love yourself first. If a boss downgraded the hard work you put into a project, love yourself first. If your spouse cheats on you, love yourself first. We all need to be our own best friends.

Take the time and figure out what will work the best for you. If you need to get a new job, or to leave a spouse, don't feel like a failure for doing it. The first thing we all need to do is be true to ourselves.

Chapter IV

Behind Those Curtains

It was 1982 and I was planning on getting married. I felt that marriage was just one of the many paths we took in life. It seemed like it was a mandatory function like paying taxes or going to school as a kid. Life was a journey and I could only move forward.

I was twenty-two years old and very unsure of myself. I had no confidence in myself and felt that I was unattractive. I had a strong case of poor self esteem. I felt that if I held out no one would be out there that would want to marry me. At the time I saw the decision in two clearly distinct ways. One was that I could have a husband, or two I could be alone the rest of my life. With those two alternatives I decided to take the life path of marriage. Usually getting married was a big event that brings much joy and happiness. Not for me, and not for my soul. A few short days prior to getting married, I had a torturous mental moment and felt a deep seated feeling of regret. Why was such a joyous moment filled with such intense regret?

At the time I did not know. At the time I was in a bathroom close to the curtains that I should have hid behind. I should have grabbed on to the curtains for dear life, for my life was about to change. Not for the better, but for the worse. I was going to marry a man that I truly had doubts about. My soul opened up when I was in that bathroom next to the curtains. That bathroom was in his basement apartment. I secretly cried a gut wrenching cry. At that time I felt that I had no one that I could confide in. I therefore just pushed away the depths of my tears and moved forward. I buried my painful, gut wrenching feelings deep inside myself. Those feelings were buried inside my soul where no one could see or touch them. I felt that I needed to straighten up and get my control back. I needed to kick my butt into gear. After all, who else would want me? I felt that if I didn't marry him no one else would want me.

I had a full blown case of poor self-esteem. It affected my soul inside and out and upside down. Did I love myself? It didn't appear that way and I certainly didn't act that way. Did I feel guilty to love myself? Did I feel that I did not deserve to love myself? Did I understand how important it was to love myself first and foremost? Those questions would eventually reappear, later in my life, when I got the diagnosis of a brain tumor. Anyway, let's talk about the marriage and some of the times that I lived through before this big event. An event that should have been a joyous time.

Let me share some of those moments, moments before I became entangled in a marriage. After I graduated nursing school in Philadelphia I headed to California. I was unsure of my future and I went out to find the meaning of life. I thought that California would be a great place to start a new life. I dreamed that it would be a wonderful place with the beautiful ocean nearby. I settled into a one bedroom apartment in Van Nuys, California. While living there I got a job at a local hospital and worked the nightshift. It was no fun trying to sleep in the daytime and be up at night to work. It was something I was not used to and my body did not like it. The hospital that I worked at was a tough place to work. One reason was the fact that the patients I took care of had some form or another of cancer. I was only twenty-one years old and felt the presence of death was looming around me in a heavy, depressing way. People died and people mourned and I felt heavy with despair. I was young and not used to this way of life. There was no room for joy, none that I was able to see in the distance.

While I had lived in California I met a man that wanted to start dating. I told him that I only wanted to be friends. My first gut reaction was to only have him as a friend. I saw many things in him that did not mesh with me. At first he listened to me and I listened to my spirit. Unfortunately, I eventually stopped listening to my spirit. After about ten months of knowing him, he again asked if we could go out as a couple again. This time I unfortunately agreed. That agreement was made over the phone, not in person. That agreement was made from one coast to the other for I had returned to Philadelphia.

I had only lived in my one bedroom apartment in California for about nine months for I was not at all happy. I did not see much of the ocean, instead I saw work and sleep. I never got used to sleeping in the daytime and always found that I was tired. I also found that I was always depressed. I constantly saw mounds of illness and death around me. I saw little happiness and joy. I had no hobbies so work became my whole life. At the time, I saw that life just equaled death. After months of this lifestyle I needed to leave for my own sake. I got into my Chevy Nova and left California. I headed straight back to Philadelphia where I had come from.

It was there in Philadelphia that I allowed myself to get caught in a difficult web. My soon to be husband left California to come to Pennsylvania where I was living. After a brief time of being together we got married. The marriage took place in my parents' home with only a few people present. Actually there were only nine people present. In other words a very small wedding.

That was the start of a trying life, a tough life, a confusing life, an all together wrong life. A life that held a question to my soul. Did I or did I not love myself?

After the marriage I went to work in a nursing home and he stayed home on the idea of doing some counseling.

He barely had a high school diploma but he felt that he would do a great job counseling. He had only one client and she was unable to pay. So, while I was out working he was at home making himself comfy watching TV and reading Star Wars books.

My money was rapidly spent by my new husband. His greediness jumped all over my paychecks as soon as I got them. His spending left little to nothing for myself. If I really loved myself would I have allowed this unfair spending of my hard earned money? Would I have allowed this unequal use of time? While I went to work and worked hard he stayed home and watched TV. Was this the life I deserved?

One thing that we did share in common was the desire to have children. After we were married we went about the process of making a child. That didn't take much effort or much pleasure. The first time I ovulated in this new marriage I became pregnant. After nine months of pregnancy we had our baby girl, a beautiful baby girl. This had brought me true happiness. I marveled at everything she did. She was the sunrise of my life.

For awhile I was not thinking about the marriage I was not thinking about myself, I was just thinking about my new baby and the joys she brought us.

Time of Reflection

I now understand why I made that big mistake of marrying my first husband. The mistake was made because I did not believe in myself. Because I had poor self-esteem I married a man that I should not have settled down with. At the time I felt that no one else would be interested in me. I was not seeing the picture correctly. First and foremost I needed to believe in myself.

I see the problem clearly now and want all my friends out there to see if they have any similar problems.

Check to see if you are in a situation that is not good for you. Check to see if the situation comes from having a poor self-esteem. Maybe you could have a better job or a better career. Maybe you could have a nicer home environment. Whatever it is, do it for yourself. Take the time and build your own temple, your own self-esteem. If it means buying nice clothes for yourself, start with that. If it means doing a hobby that you enjoy, start with that. Whatever it is, do it for yourself. It leads us in the right direction if we take the time to love ourselves first.

Chapter V

Functioning in the Daily Routines of a Married Life

The daily routines in my married life weighed me down hour by hour, minute by minute. I worked full time and my husband didn't work at all. I worked until two days before my daughter Alice was born. Six weeks after the birth of my first child I went back to work. Who else would work? My husband did not work. He would get a job for a few weeks to a month and then lose it. He was not a dependable employee. That did not worry him a bit for he knew that he could count on me. He could count on my paychecks. The role of the breadwinner was mine. That was not my only role in that marriage. I soon took on other roles. I was the housekeeper, the laundress, the gardener, the bill payer etc.

Marriage was nothing that it was cracked up to be but having a baby was a gift that was priceless. I enjoyed being a mother. I wanted to give her nothing but the best. I decided to breast feed her since that was the healthiest and most natural way to go. I was still nursing my daughter when I returned to work in six weeks, so I started to express my milk. I saved it for her so she could have that natural healthy milk even when I was at work. During my meal break at work I would lock myself up in the bathroom. I would use that time to express the milk from my breasts. I felt that I was doing the right thing by providing the nutritious food my daughter needed. She was finally introduced to baby food around the age of six months. She didn't like it at first but soon got used to it. By the age of two she was completely weaned from breast milk and on a regular diet.

Yes, I did say two years of age when she was totally weaned from breast feeding. I will admit that breast feeding was not a thing to do in my family. My brother and I were both bottle fed. Was breast feeding a bad thing to do? No, not to me. I continued to do it. I kind of kept it under raps and did it very privately. Though I might have seemed like an easy pushover, I had strong beliefs on certain things. I did what felt right to me. I had the strength to follow through on some of my convictions. The one thing I was weak on was loving myself. I fell very short in that area. I remembered that I had fallen short in that area for as long as I could remember. It was a feeling that I had grown up with. In time I needed to realize that I could change that feeling.

Even though I struggled to love myself I loved my new daughter. I loved how cute she looked. I loved her movements. I loved her way of communicating. Everything she did I saw as marvelous. I thought that every outfit on her was adorable . It was a very happy time for me. I had been clueless as to how wonderful that experience could be. It was the first adventure in my life that made me happy. Work and marriage were just chores for me.

I was slowly learning that marriage was just a huge weight on my shoulders. One time a physician told me that I looked like I was lugging a heavy weight on my bony shoulders. Little did he know how right he was. Anyway this married life of mine continued. I continued to work and my husband continued to stay at home. I made the money and he spent the money. He dropped the dirty clothes on the floor and I picked them up and cleaned them. He used the dishes and I washed them. He dropped the crumbs and I swept them. It was an endless race to keep the home we lived in clean. It was an endless race for me to keep up with the finances.

The money situation in that marriage never matured into a peaceful adult compromise. As I said before I continued to work and he continued to stay at home. I wanted to save money and he wanted to spend money. When I came into the marriage I had ten thousand dollars to my name. Within eight years of marriage I had ten thousand dollars of debt to my name. He used credit cards like fire trucks use water. There was no end in site. I would sit up alone some nights working on the bills while everyone else slept. It was a huge burden to me. I felt that I was trapped in my own prison.

I never spent any money on myself. I wore old clothes and cut my own hair. I wore no makeup. I was just a plain Jane and thought I was unattractive. My husband never complimented me. Instead he would deflate my sense of self. Did he really love me? Did I really love myself?

This unhappiness continued for eight years but after sometime I decided that I needed a divorce. I felt unhappy and over burdened. I learned through all of this turmoil, that we cannot change how other people act or behave. We do not have the power to change other people. I would try to talk to him and ask him to help clean up around the house. I would talk to him and ask him to be more careful with spending the money, but no matter how much was spoken nothing changed. The same patterns continued. I was getting to the point of being pushed over the edge. I carried too much weight and I needed to do something to end it.

He knew how to control me so when I mentioned the word divorce he took pills. He consciously or unconsciously knew that this would have a huge effect on me. He said that he would kill himself and that scared me. I quickly stopped any plans for a divorce. We continued on with our life with no changes. I continued to work and he continued to spend my money while he stayed at home doing nothing.

Two years later something strange but powerful happened to me. While I was turning the hot and cold water knobs in the shower something came to me. It came to me as clear as day. It came out of nowhere, and it was a deep insight. The insight showed me that I needed to get a divorce to save myself. I needed to love myself first and standup for myself. I did not have to wait for someone to love me. I needed to move on for me. I needed to realize that I was a worthy person, and needed to be comfortable with myself.

I then went into high gear and started to plan this event secretly. I met with a lawyer at lunchtime. I had lied and told my husband that I was going out to lunch with some friends. I talked over the details with the lawyer and she told me her price. It took me many months to save the money but I was determined. I was going for a no-fault divorce and planned on leaving my husband in a comfortable way. This time he took things well for I had everything paid for and I gave him the better deal. In a few months the arrangement of that horrible marriage was dissolved.

Not everything in that marriage was a horrible thing for there were three joyful things that came out of it. During that marriage I had three children. Those three kids were my biggest gifts. I would get pregnant when the youngest one was about two years old. Sex wasn't anything important to me at the time so I was blessed with the ease of becoming pregnant. I would ovulate, have intercourse, and that would become a baby. I was a fertile Myrtle and a frigid woman all at the same time. I conceived as easily as rabbits did. It didn't matter that I was a frigid woman, for that part of my body still made babies. I often would inwardly blame myself for the frigid part. I kept that knowledge deeply buried in my heart. Later on in life things changed for the better. It was a good change, a change that I could never have even imagined.

Time of Reflection

It took so much strength for me to go through the proceedings of a divorce. Even though it was the right thing to do, I felt like I had failed. I felt like a divorce was a failing grade on a report card. It made me question myself. The truth was that the problems in that marriage were very real. If I did not look at them directly they could have destroyed me. I now look back and feel thankful that I had the strength to go through with the divorce.

Friends, please do what you feel is the right thing to do. Trust in yourself. We usually can feel the truth. It often comes at unannounced, quiet moments in our lives. For me it came when I was in the bathroom adjusting the water for my shower. I believe that the truth is out there for all of us to explore. The truth comes when we believe and love ourselves.

Chapter VI

A Difficult Matrimony

We all take many journeys in our lives and some are not so positive. My first marriage was a difficult journey. A journey that could have taken the life out of me, a journey that showed no love for myself. Only after the divorce was I clearly able to see how things went down. When in a situation it is hard to really see it clearly. Things that are so close come in cloudily. It wasn't until afterwards that I saw the pain it caused me. I saw how poorly I was treated as a human being. Why did I let him treat me in an unkind way? Why did I not take time for myself? Why was I the only one that had a job and made money? Why was I the only one that cleaned the house? Why did I allow such unhappiness to continue?

The divorce after my first marriage was a difficult time to go through even through it was the right thing for me to do. I do not think that divorces are good times for anybody. It was a stressful time no matter how it was sliced. It was a dramatic life change and that brought new learning experiences with it. I did get into counseling and started to take antidepressant medication. During this time I had to rediscover myself. I had to start over again. I had to learn that I needed to love myself first. I had to learn how to love me for me.

After awhile I settled into a home, in a quiet area. It was not a very industrious area so the prices of the homes were way below average. The area that I lived in used to get its economic diet from the coal business but that had long ago died off. Homes were dirt cheap and that is what I could afford. In that area I raised my two sons. My daughter had chosen to live with her father at that time. He lived in the projects about seventeen miles away. He was living off of the government. He could no longer live off of me, so he conveniently started to live off the government.

I kept busy with working and raising my two sons. We were busy with Cub Scouts and Boy Scouts and other fun things boys like to do. Life seemed to have settled down at that time.

After sometime another man came into my life. This man was very different compared to my first husband . He worked and he worked. He had a history of working and supporting his family in his first marriage. He usually worked as a laborer in factories, so the income level was low, but it was at least dependable. He even worked around the house doing small jobs. He would do landscaping outside, and be a handyman in the house. He did everything from moving radiators in the house, to putting up wallpaper, to cutting down big trees outside. He was very dependable in that way.

He also had moments of being helpful with my sons. He taught both of them how to hunt and fish. My youngest son got his first deer at the age of twelve with his guidance. I felt that the experiences with this man helped both my boys become men. I appreciated that down deep. Anyone who helped my children was special to me. Through all of those wonderful activities there was something wrong, something secretly looming. A dark cloud was hanging over head. A cloud that eventually took all the sunshine out of the day. A once sunny day became a dark dreary day. The overcast was alcohol.

I did not know that he was an alcoholic when I had first met him. I was unfamiliar with alcohol since it was not in my history nor in my family's history. My family hardly touched it so I was never even exposed to the whole meaning of the world of alcoholism. He had done a fine job of hiding it from me when we first met. He was a secret closet drinker and I did not even suspect it. He finally did admit it later and he went into rehab. I supported him through the whole process and even went to AA meetings with him. It was a learning experience for me. He did stay sober for a total of seven years. I knew that it was a daily struggle inside his soul, but he kept the fight up for those seven years, seven long years. The time though was quickly coming to an end, an ugly end.

In the month of July, a few weeks before my middle son James was due to join the Army, my second husband had a fight with him. It was a day to enjoy and rejoice in not one to choke on with despair, but things happen. On that beautiful sunny day my second husband had an axe in his hand and was pushing up against my son James. They were outside in the yard on what was a beautiful summer day. I saw the whole episode explode right before my eyes.

It started off with my husband at the time, having a loud banter with my son. He was angry and acting mean. I listened to the loud words that were exchanged between the two of them. I felt that my second husband was in the wrong and I spoke up and verbally supported James. I calmly told my husband to stop what he was doing. James, at that time, was a boy becoming a man and he kept his ground. He could no longer be pushed around by an adult. My husband became even angrier because I had verbally supported my son. He dropped the axe with a deep thud on the innocent green grass and marched up to me. He glared at me straight into my eyes with anger and hatred. It appeared that he despised me. His eyes were bulging out of his face with wrath. A face that I had unfortunately seen too many times before. In a few short sentences mixed heavily with foul language he spit out his anger toward me. He told me right then and there that the marriage was over. He moved out that day and alcohol moved back in with him.

We were divorced in no time. It probably sounded too sudden to get a divorce over such a small little fight, on a warm sunny day, but there had been webs of cold darkness drawn prior to that day. He did not like that I paid attention to my sons. He actually seemed jealous of the affection I showered on my sons. He seemed to unconsciously try to limit the time I spent with my sons. It appeared like he wanted to own all of my time. He had a strange way of controlling me and I was too close to the situation to see it with my naked eyes.

At first we had lived together not being legally married. After a few short years without being married we decided to make it official and got married. After we were officially married for one year he mentioned the D word. He mentioned the word *divorce*. I was shocked at that thought for I truly had believed that we were going to be married until be were peacefully put into the ground. After hearing that word I put on a protective coat of armor. I had to take care of myself. I had to plan for my children. I had to love myself.

I secretly started saving money in a safety deposit box. I worked and used most of my money to keep us going jointly, but I kept reserves secretly stashed away. I used the regular money for necessities but kept the extra as my needed lifeline. I kept it well hidden. Two years later after he had first mentioned the word divorce he had that ugly fight with my son James. My caution was then used to help me out. I had to pay off my ex-husband to keep the house we lived in. I needed a place to live in and thankfully I had one. I was saved by my own secretly stored money. My sons and I were taken care of due to my secretive savings.

A big problem loomed over me for I felt like a failure again. I had two divorces to my name. I must have been a pretty awful woman to be the owner of two divorce decrees. I must have been a failure. I felt embarrassed by this history and tried to keep it hidden. Where I worked I had people believe that I had only been married and divorced once. Since I wasn't that close to my coworkers they did not need to know the whole ugly truth about me. All the girls at work, except one, were married. Everyone there was still married to their first husband. I lived in an area where divorce was a rarity and gossip was a common practice. I therefore kept most of my life a secret. I even kept the fact that my heritage was Jewish for the neighborhood I lived in would not tolerate that. I kept many things a secret. Where were these secrets kept? Did I keep them in my heart? Did I keep them in the recesses of my brain? I would never know, but they were kept deeply buried.

Time of Reflection

To this day I am proud of myself for standing up for my own son. I have no regrets that my actions probably caused the start of my second divorce. Down deep I knew that it would happen one day anyway.

To all the parents out there ,trust in your parenting skills. There will be many trials out there. Being a parent is not always an easy job. Just love yourself and through that you will love your children. I did it a bit backwards. I loved my children first and through that I was able to love myself.

Chapter VII

Life After Divorce

After the second divorce I spent most of my time and energy on my children. At the time of my diagnosis of a brain tumor, I had only one child still living at home with me. My daughter was on her own with her three kids and my middle son was married and in the service. Everyone was growing up quickly. My kids grew into adults far too fast for me but I had no way of slowing it down. Before I could even ponder about the empty nest syndrome I decided to hang on to my youngest son Joel. I was scared of the thought of an empty nest. I felt that I had a good life with my kids and the thought of being alone was scary. It would be a whole new world to me, and the new world seemed dreadfully lonely.

During this time I would still see my second ex for brief periods of time. Even though we were divorced he still wanted to see me.

I would give in and see him but they were not good moments. He would earnestly tell me that he wanted to get back together with me and that he still loved me. I would start to trust him again just to have that trust broken. He would be with me for one moment and the next moment he would be back with his new girlfriend.

The new girlfriend was more acquainted with alcohol and so I felt they were a much better match. Also both of them smoked. Cigarette smoking was taken to the deepest level of their lungs. They shared that too since I never smoked. I had met her several times so I knew her enough to hold conversations with her. I personally didn't like her scheming ways but I kept things on the up and up. I was friendly and polite. She knew her new boyfriend still had feelings for his ex-wife and I could sense that it bothered her. She wanted to control him and after sometime she won the race. She got him tightly wrapped around her fingers, the same fingers that held her cigarettes.

It took me a total of four years after that divorce to be dissolved of the love and the hate that marriage caused. After four years I just wished for him to have a safe and happy life and I moved on. Even though he lived less than two miles from me I just let things dissolve. I no longer looked to see if his car was parked where they lived. I had moved on. I had moved on in a positive way. I was learning to love myself.

After the divorce I was free to spend my time and my money as I wanted to. Alice, my oldest child, was more than ready to take the help. She needed lots of help. She needed lots of financial help. She needed lots of help cleaning the apartments she lived in. She just plain needed help. She would be moving from place to place and needed money all the time. Alice was not working and I felt responsible for her children.

The fathers of her first two were of no help. The first father lived incognito to escape from the required child support dollars. He once was in prison for not paying child support but soon learned how to trick the system. I do not know where he is to this day and neither does his own son. The second man pays his child support but that is all he pays. He lives very close, miles wise, to his son but he shows no interest. He does not even see his son. It is a sad situation all around. My last grandchild from my daughter broke the pattern. The father of this child really cares about his daughter. He and his family take the child about forty percent of the time. They spend time with her and truly love her. To me that is a gift and I am thankful for that.

There were so many problems in my daughter's life that I could not even begin to solve them. I felt her heavy load and felt I had the responsibility to resolve something. The one thing I felt I could resolve was her living quarters. I needed to buy a home for her and her three children. I took what little money I had and I bought a small inexpensive dwelling for her and the kids to live in. It was small with a postage stamp sized backyard but it worked. It was noisy at her house because it was right next to a car wash but it was a home. It had a living room, dining room, kitchen, three bedrooms and a bathroom. She settled into the home and I continued to help her. I paid for the water and the sewer bills, I paid the taxes on the house, I paid the trash bill and most of all I paid the mortgage payment. It was a drain on me, but I knew how to deny myself of things. I had long ago learned those skills. I had learned them way back when I lived with my first husband. I did not go on vacations, I did not go to restaurants, I did not buy myself new clothes. I lived on a tight rope and made it work. I learned how to go to the Good-Will store to buy clothes. I did not go to a hairdresser, I cut my own hair. I drank my juice half water half juice to save money. It was a constant effort but I was making it work for my children.

My middle son was in the service and he had learned to make his own way in life. He was a bigger help to me than he realized. He did not take advantage of me. He went into boot camp at the tender age of seventeen and turned eighteen while he was in his training. He had learned at a young age how to take care of himself and how to count on himself. He was a man before I could even say "boo."

Now my youngest and very dear son was home with me. He was extremely intelligent but not yet mature enough to make wise decisions. He wanted to try everything in life and enjoy life to its fullest. With all of his zest for life he did run into problems with the police force. Throughout his growing up years I probably spent more money than I can count. It cost a bunch of money just to clean up some of the messes he got into. I spent on him in a different way than I spent on his sister. The spending on them did not allow me to spend on myself. My Joel was also the one that was going to college. I saved every red cent that I could for his college. I planned on paying for the whole thing by myself without any school loans. I planned on doing it completely independently for nothing was going to come from his father. His father, who lived off the government, never even dreamed of helping his son pay for college.

I was busy making life work and I kept busy working at it. I did not have time to become sick. I had things to do. I had things to accomplish. I was so busy working and helping my children that I didn't have anytime for a thing called a tumor. When that horrible diagnosis came my way I was not at all ready for it. I usually liked to plan for things, but the tumor didn't let me plan. It had its own frame of time. The tumor set my whole life back. It took me by surprise and knocked me over. What had I done to deserve this golf ball sized tumor nestled in my head? Was the tumor my fault? Did I cause it to grow in the recesses of my brain? This was something I needed to understand, something I needed to learn about. I needed to explore my whole life to try and to get a glimpse of understanding.

Time of Reflection

I now realize that giving and giving is not always the right thing to do. The more I gave to Alice the more she took. I knew Alice needed help but the more help I gave her the more help she needed. It was a never ending saga. Was I doing the wrong thing? Was I harming myself? Was I stopping her from learning on her own?

35

I now understand that helping someone isn't always the right thing to do. For example let's say you are helping someone with a drug or alcohol problem, is it the right thing to do? I guess there are times that they really could use the help, but then there are other times that your help keeps them trapped in their own problems. In some circumstances it might be better to just let things happen and let that person pull on their own strength from inside. By doing that it might change their lives.

I knew a parent that kicked his son out the door because that son had a big drug addiction. The interesting thing was that the son recovered on his own and is now leading a very productive life. Maybe the son learned to love himself over the drugs. I can now understand that we sometimes need to allow an individual to fly on his or her own. It might take courage to let them go, but sometimes it is the right thing to do.

Chapter VIII

Returning Home

In the month of May in 2007 my daughter Alice, her two sons, and her new baby daughter came home to my house. My first granddaughter, a cute little baby girl named Gene was coming home. Luckily I was let out of the hospital, so that I could be in my own home. I was given time to plan for the future of my brain tumor. I was able to go home and be there for my daughter when she was discharged from the hospital. She needed me at that time in her life. With three children she needed lots of help. She needed a pile of help in every which way.

I was given time which was so desperately needed during those hectic hours and days. At the time my brain tumor had to take a back seat on the bus, and wait patiently until I was ready to deal with it. I had no time to ponder over its presence. I needed to store away my worry about my diagnosis. The tumor was pushed back into the warm ominous area of brain that it dominated. I had more important things to do. I had a new granddaughter to shower with love along with enjoying her two older brothers.

We all came home to a warm inviting place that was well kept. That was my home, my home sweet home. A place so special to go to after such a heavy diagnosis of a brain tumor.

During that time things were really hectic. I wasn't feeling up to snuff but I was thankful that I was able to function. I did the cleaning, and the cooking, and the entertaining of the guests that came to see the new baby. I did whatever I could to be helpful to everyone living in my house. Luckily, at the time, I was able to carry the load of being the head of the household. I was able to carry that load, and the load that was stored inside my head.

Out in my living room, on a pulled out sofa sleeper, was a warm comfortable spot for the new mom, my daughter. Having been cut in the abdomen to remove the new life caused difficult moments. The muscles and the tissues in her belly were sore and needed time to heal. It was difficult for her to move around much but things slowly started their healing processes.

Her other older two children were busy running around the house, being kids. They felt the chaotic energy in the house and ran free with it. Their new sister helped with this scattered energy for she was up at least every two hours. She needed to be fed, diapered, and held softly for love. Getting sleep was just a borrowed luxury for short periods of time. My neat orderly house became a cluttered mess. There were clothes, unused disposable diapers of various sizes, kids' toys, and gift wrap scattered everywhere. It was a mess and her two older sons rejoiced in the clutter.

Also in the house was my youngest son Joel, who was eighteen years old at the time. He had his own events of activity going on in his life for he was soon to graduate from high school. Graduation was a big event for it was the completion of our standard education. He was busy planning for his new life ahead of him. He had things to do and thoughts to ponder over. Energy seemed to be bursting through every crevice of the house. It was not a time to rest for anyone in my house.

The following month of June things finally calmed down. My daughter and her three kids went back to their own house. I stared to reclaim my house and had done a complete cleaning. Each item in the house was back to its resting place and was as clean as it used to be. The house felt better and more relaxed but I wasn't. I was feeling drained both physically and mentally. I felt that I was more tired than usual and felt that I couldn't do all the work that I use to do. I had returned to my job, but I knew that it was only temporary for I needed to do something about my health. I now had the time to think about myself. I found it depressing to think about that golf ball sized tumor nestled in my head. There was no happiness pondering over that miserable thing.

The time ticked away and it came time for me to make a solid decision. I could no longer ignore my brain tumor. I wished that it didn't exist but it did. It continued to loom in my head with its own presence. I needed to do something, so in that month of June, I went down to Philadelphia. Two of my friends and I hopped in a car and headed south. I lived in the coal region of Pennsylvania which was about three hours away from Philadelphia. I thought that Philly would have my answer. I figured that a busy metropolis would have the answer I was looking for. I wanted someone with expertise to tell me what I needed to do to get rid of that thing called a tumor.

After much driving around Philly we finally found a parking space and parked the car. We then walked into the huge prominent building standing high against the sky. I was there to find the answer. When we finally got in the presence of the doctor all of us listened to every word that came from the neurosurgeon's mouth. He was not as tall as I expected and spoke rather quietly.

The sad thing was, I was not given a direct answer. I wanted an answer but instead I was given three choices. I could do nothing, have radiation, or have surgery. Of course, if I did nothing the tumor would take over and stop my respirations. It was pushing into some high real-estate in my brain. Though it was not cancerous it would have the same end result, which was death if I did nothing. It would probably be a slow and scary death, and at the time I was terrified of my own death. Therefore doing nothing was not an answer I could accept.

My other two options were radiation or surgery. I didn't want to have the responsibly to make my own decision but I had to. I wished the powers of above could have told me what to do. I looked at the easiest treatment and that was to have a procedure called gamma knife radiation. My tumor was almost too large for this procedure but the doctor assured me that it was workable. With hesitation and reluctance I decided that I would go that route.

The following week I went back to Philadelphia for the gamma knife radiation treatment. The plan was for the radiation to shrink that terrible growth in my head. It was a one time deal and I wanted to get it over with quickly. The quicker the better. I had other things in life to worry about besides that nasty thing called a tumor.

Early one morning, still in the month of June, my friend and I arrived at the outpatient department for the gamma knife radiation treatment. There were two other patients there in that department. They too were there for this new type of radiation. Both of them appeared satisfied with what was about to happen to them. Even though I did not feel confident we were there together for the same reason. I felt that we shared something in common and that made me feel like they were just old friends of mine. None of us had ever met before but at this moment we shared a common path in life.

The staff in that department came to me and told me to put on the regular attire of a hospitalized patient. I took off my street clothes and slipped into that not so glamorous blue and white gown. The staff then had me climb onto a stretcher. After some time of just lying silently on the stretcher they wheeled me into a room with blocked off walls.

That particular room had very thick walls that were too scientific for me to understand. I did know that it was necessary to keep the radiation contained within those four fat walls. The radiation had a job to do and a path to take. The radiation was going to be steered into my head. The tumor was going to be the radiation's center of attention. I was strapped down with a helmet on my head that was full of small holes. It was important that I didn't move. I was not to move even the slightest. The radiation was to go only to the places it was guided to. The room with the thick walls was quiet and full of solitude. I was there alone with my enemy the brain tumor. Together we were lying there still and as quiet as a mouse. I inwardly hoped that the spirit from above was there too.

Every once in a while, through an intercom, I would hear one of the doctors asking how I was doing. I didn't have any discomfort only a feeling of uncertainty. I therefore told them that I was fine, which was just half of the truth. I was feeling alone in a room with invisible things jumping into my head. It was half sci-fi and half primitive. After nine unfelt jolts the procedure was completed. In a way it felt like nothing had been done. In reality a mini universe had been created. Radiation had passed into my head and I didn't know the future of its effects.

I was then wheeled back to the starting point in the other room. There I was watched over by a nurse. She took my vital signs and monitored how I was doing. I felt fine and everything appeared normal. I was lying there anxiously awaiting to be discharged. In a short time my street clothes were returned to me. I quickly removed the hospital gown and put on my own attire. I was feeling thankful that the procedure was over with and just wanted to go home. Maybe I was done worrying about a tumor. Maybe something good had happened. Something major had truly happened and it happened very quietly.

My friend, who was with me, was the designated driver. We had made that agreement prior to coming to the gamma knife procedure. We walked out of the tall oppressive walls of the hospital into the sunshine. I was no longer in a room behind thick walls, I was out in the open. I felt weak walking back to her car so I got into the back seat. I could lie down in the back seat and that is what I planned on doing.

On the way home my friend was hungry, so we stopped at a rest stop that had a restaurant. I saw nothing that I was hungry for, but felt that I should eat something since I had had nothing for the last sixteen hours. I decided on getting chicken soup. I figured that it would make me feel better. Chicken soup always got a high rating for helping people feel better. Once I got the cup of soup I stated to feel even worse. I managed to get into a chair at the restaurant. I felt like putting my head down to my knees but did not want to appear strange out in public at the restaurant. I kept feeling worse by the minute, I forced myself to take three spoonfuls of soup. That was the only thing that made it down my throat. I felt too sick to eat. My friend on the other hand ate away with pleasure; her appetite was good and as strong as a horse. Food felt much more welcomed and accepted around her than by me. I sat there at the restaurant while she finished her food. I just hung on to the moment and swallowed my own saliva.

Walking back to her car was also a struggle. When we finally reached her car I climbed back into the back seat. She made sure I was comfortable and started back on the journey heading home. The motion of her vehicle made my stomach feel even sicker and I felt that I would soon vomit. My friend did not want a drop of vomit in her car so when the urge to vomit came I hung my head halfway into a plastic bag. Vomit erupted a number of times. I neatly upchucked into the bag for I did not want to upset my friend. The vomit neatly keep itself tucked into the plastic bag.

The interesting thing was that no one had told me that I would feel sick after the radiation treatment. Maybe it was just me, who knew? Maybe my body was more sensitive than others. Maybe it was too much radiation in my head for my body to handle. Maybe my body was rebelling from the sci-fi prehistoric treatment it received. This was left to be unanswered.

Two days after the procedure I returned to work, after all, I had to work. I had always worked and made my own money to survive. I needed to pay those darn bills, just like so many of us have to do. Work went on and I went on even though I did not feel well. I pretended that all was going well. My body did not always let me pretend. I would have days that I felt horrible. I would feel weak and have terrible pains in my head. Some days just moving a few steps was difficult. Was that supposed to happen?

One weekend, in the month of September, I had such intense pain in my head. It became so bad that I had a hard time just to function in the everyday activities of life. I decided to drive myself to the hospital. That was quite unusual for me because I usually avoided hospitals even though I worked in one. Anyway the pain would not let me go onward so with some regret I did go to the hospital. It took a great amount of concentration to drive my car. I made it there with my well trained hand and foot motions for they had been trained for years to operate a stick shift. My Honda, Civic made her way to the hospital almost all on her own. She made all the stops and made all the correct turns. She, yes I called her a she, took me there safely.

While I was at the hospital I had to answer your typical questions. I had to hand in my insurance card and provide that type of information. I was given Tylenol and left alone on a stretcher. Again I was left alone on yet another narrow stretcher. I was again left to lie alone behind some non descript curtains. I had gotten use to lying behind curtains and looking at them while questioning my life. In that ER nothing was really taken seriously and I was given prescriptions for drugs and sent home. Little did I know, at the time, that I would wind up living on drugs. I would take drugs just to function in the daily routines of life.

The drugs became my life partners. I had never taken drugs so this was a very different experience for me. I lived on the drugs for the next nine months of my life. One on them being a narcotic called Percocet, also called Oxycodone /APAP. Another was a steroid called Decadron. I also added Tylenol into the mix to assist with the pain control. I did not know that I would suffer so much from the Gamma Knife Radiation treatment. If I would have known I never would have chosen that option.

Was that supposed to happen? Was I supposed to suffer every minute I breathed? Was pain destined to become my companion? The only thing that I did know was that I had to keep going. I had to keep going even if it was only from hour to hour, minute to minute.

Time of Reflection

Friends, that was an extremely hard time for me and I suffered to my core. I still have watery eyes when I explain it to you. I questioned my own existence. At the time I only half existed and needed the flow of faith and love into my soul. The depth of that pain only makes me want to encourage you and tell you that I love you.

Chapter IX

Living on Percocet

I had a change in life after I had the Gamma Knife Radiation treatment. The change was not for the better. I was living on many pills. It became a way of life for me after the radiation. I had no idea that life would become so difficult after I had that treatment. I had been told that it could take awhile for the treatment to work so I figured I just had to wait and suffer in silence. I knew that I wasn't a patient person so I scolded myself to be patient with the recovery.

For someone that had never lived on pills before, I got used to swallowing those chemical agents every few hours. A couple of swallows a day kept the doctor away and eased the constant pain. I lived in pain and the medication barely kept me functioning. I went to work, cleaned my house, and paid my bills. Those were the only things that I could accomplish, and that was with much difficulty. The rest of the time I just hibernated. I laid on the couch in my living room to vegetate. I was not able to do anything else. Each activity was a struggle and therefore I limited my life as much as I could. Lying on the couch became my salvation. In some ways I became a hermit.

The ugly steroid pills made me bloat up like a balloon. I quickly gained about fifteen to twenty pounds of fat that mostly accumulated around my mid section. I had a fat face for a woman that had always had a thin face. I had a fat neck and chin, and my belly was embarrassingly chubby. I wore loose clothes to hide my new ugly figure. I even stopped wearing a bra because my bras were too tight on me. I looked like a new woman in a few short months. A totally unhealthy and uncomfortably larger woman. A woman that I could hardly look at in the mirror. I became a woman that I could hardly recognized. I was a woman trying to live day by day with a mean tumor renting room in her brain.

I continued to sleep at night and wake up and go to work in the daytime. It was a limited life. It was an unpleasant life. In October, a few months after the radiation treatment, someone openly admitted to me that they noticed that things were different with me. She had the courage to mention that I was not myself. She noticed that I walked at a much slower pace. She noticed that I stopped having a smile flow across my face. I did open up and share a small portion of my struggles with her. She felt that I should try and get off of work. I did not see that as a possibility for I had to work. I had to work to keep my house, I had to work to keep food in my refrigerator, I had to work to keep saving for my son's college. Since I was the sole money maker I had to keep working no matter what. I had to push myself to keep moving to do that four letter word they call work.

Alone, I took on the weight of the world and balanced it precariously on my shoulders. Some of the weight was for my children. One of my goals was to send my youngest child to college. He had the intelligence and I believed in him completely. I wanted to be his helper for I loved him to the core. The father of that child did nothing to help. No money came from him and no encouragement came either. The father of my three children had remarried and was living off of the governments' money. In other words, he just collected. He did not give a cent to his children. He did not even attend his son's high school graduation even though he only lived half an hour away. He didn't even give his son moral support to go to college. Sending my son to college was completely in my lap, and I was happy to do it.

I did not share my burdens with my fellow workers. I did not share the information that I took pain medication. My pain and my medications were my secret business. I figured that work would judge me negatively for taking narcotics. I therefore kept that information secretly hidden. I drove my car and did everything that I had done before, while I swallowed pill after pill. I was not addicted but needed to down those pills to function. At times I would try and decrease the dose of the Decadron but I would end up with such intense pain in my head that life became unbearable. The pain also did not let me limit the use of Percocets. I did try but the attempts ended with extreme pain. Living became nothing but a struggle. Percocets became as necessary as oxygen is to breathe. Decadrons became as necessary as food in the stomach. The gamma knife radiation had only made my life worse. For all of those months after I had the radiation treatment each day became a struggle to survive.

Time of Reflection

I am not ashamed to admit that I was on narcotics. They were needed for survival at the time. Today I do not take a single pill but back then they were a necessary friend. I needed them just to function.

Friends, please do not feel inferior or mad at yourself if you need help of any kind. Some people need Chiropractic treatment, some need pills, some need a relaxing vacation and others just need plain attention. Whatever it is, accept what you need at the present time.

Chapter X

Many Months Later

After eleven months I knew that the gamma knife radiation had not done anything to help me. It probably had hurt me more than it had helped me. My tumor made up it's mind and was not going to recede in size. I needed to take drastic measures and change things. I went to a large hospital and saw a neurosurgeon. I had a meeting with one of the surgeons, the head of the department. I was very fortunate that he was the head of the department, for I believed he was the best and most qualified doctor to go into the recesses of my brain.

He was blunt and to the point. He told me that I would be dead within three to five years if I did not have the tumor removed. It was located in high real-estate and would eventually stop my body from the simple act of breathing. It was located near the center that controlled breathing. Yes, it was non-cancerous but it had no business occupying space in my head. It could kill me, and it coldly told me of its intentions. I did not take much time to make a decision. I just wanted it out. The tumor was the size of a golf ball and it did not belong in my head. It was slowly eating me away. I watched as my body slowly lost its strength on my right side. I started lifting things with my left side due to my right sided weakness. The tumor was slowly ticking away at the time. It was slowly debilitating me. It was slowly taking away my life.

I went into high gear and decided to have the surgery. I let work know about my surgery and planned accordingly. I must have known something for I took everything away from work. I did not even leave one pen there. I took all of my stuff and packed it away. I did all of the work that I could do ahead of time to make my job easier for someone that would be taking over. I worked on my staffs' schedules so it would be completed for months to come. I completed my work and then some. I left with no stone unturned. Maybe my soul knew more than I knew at the time. That was often a true thing in my life. One's soul sees things clearer than they do. Maybe my soul knew about things to come, but thankfully I did not. Maybe I was fortunate that I did not know what was coming.

I wanted the tumor out and I wanted it out now. I had waited for a total of eleven months after the gamma knife radiation and my patience had run out. The gamma knife radiation treatment was a sour defeat and I had to move forward. My surgery was scheduled for two weeks after meeting with the surgeon. I went into the hospital the day before the surgery to get my scalp shaved and marked. No one was going to play hop-scotch on my head, but they needed it marked for placement, the games were just about ready to begin.

The morning of the procedure I was driven to the hospital by my middle child, my other wonderful son, who had traveled far to be with me. He had been fighting overseas in a not so nice war. He was in the army and was in military police. He left me there and wished me well. I just sat in the waiting room waiting for them to call my name. Many other folks were in the room and each of us were there for different reasons. I looked like no one special and looked like nothing big was about to happen. Well, something huge was about to happen. It was going to happen to me—a girl that looked unhappy and steroid dependent, a girl that had barely existed for the past eleven months of her life. That girl was me.

I knew that this was not going to be a simple surgery and wondered if the doctor felt a bit uneasy. He had told me that it was going to be a difficult surgery. He said it would be an eight out of a ten difficulty. It wasn't until I saw him later that he told me my surgery was a nine point five out of ten. It turned out to be harder than he thought it would be. My surgery took a grueling long eight hours. I wondered if anyone had time to eat lunch or go to the bathroom during those unpleasant eight hours. It didn't matter to me since I was asleep under general anesthesia. I was in a deep sleep. I was close to the other side but still here on this earth. I was somewhere, where, I do not know. I am thankful that I do not remember.

Time of Reflection

The one lesson that I learned from this whole experience was that we have to keep on trying. If one fails at something do not give up. Stand up and try something else. My gamma knife radiation was a huge failure so I needed to try something else. I could not give up. I had to keep moving forward. It looked dark and gloomy to me at the time but I could only move in one direction. I could only move forward. Having surgery was the last thing I wanted to do but it was something I had to do. I had to do it if I wanted to stay alive. Having my youngest son still living with me was a huge push for me to go forward. I wanted to be around for him.

Dear friends out there, no matter how difficult things are out there, please keep trying. Do it for yourself.

Chapter XI

Post Op

After the surgery I didn't remember much. I do remember being in the ICU and having the nurses turn me on my side to change a sheet under me. I briefly remember my three children visiting me. I remember my mother visiting me once and a friend along with her husband came to visit. Most of it was a blur. I remember pain and that days turned into nights, but that was all that I remembered.

It wasn't until I was at the rehab part of the hospital that my memory started to slowly kick back into place. My mind wasn't fully working but it kept trying. In that department I had a roommate, a woman in her eighties. She had broken her hip and was there for rehabilitation. She seemed to get a lot of attention and I kind of felt ignored. I found that sleeping was the best way to pass the time. I wanted the time to pass so that I could go back to my own environment, my own home. I did not feel like I was on vacation being away from home. I felt like I was in prison. I was in a small space in an enclosed environment.

I was limited in what I was allowed to do. The simplest things in life were not permitted. One example was going to the bathroom. I remember that I had tried to go the bathroom twice on my own and each time I ended up falling on the floor. My mind didn't really comprehend why my body didn't walk right. The nurses that found me on the floor were not at all happy with me and scolded me for my act. My mind was not yet used to the fact that I could not do such simple acts. I could not even walk twelve feet to the bathroom. I felt stupid and childish. I didn't want anyone to know that I had done this "no no." I felt like I was a bad girl. "Shame on me", was my inward thought. I was mad at myself for some unexplainable reason. The idea that I was incapable to do even the simplest of activities had not yet settled into my thinking.

During the day I was placed in a wheelchair and taken to the physical therapy department. It was there that I slowly realized what was wrong with me. It was there in their rehab department that harsh reality snuck up and hit me in the brain. A brain that had a huge operation. Just sitting there in the wheelchair gave me time to reassess all that I had been through.

One thing that came clear to my thought process was the fact that I had double vision and had to wear an eye patch over my left eye. It was my left eye since the surgery took place on the left side of my brain. The tumor was left and center so they entered my skull on the left side. Being that it was such a difficult surgery my optic nerve got too close to the surgeon's blade. It was severed and unfortunately there was no way to repair it. It left me with double vision. I never blamed the surgeon for this blunder for I knew he had an extremely difficult surgery to perform. I had not initially realized that I had double vision after the surgery since my left eye was swollen shut. After the surgery I was bruised from the top of my head, down my face, and into my neck. I looked like I had been in a battle and lost and in many ways. I truly had lost.

While there in the physical therapy department I relearned who I now was. I was a crippled girl that only saw out of one eye. I could hardly walk. I had to relearn how to walk. I had to relearn the simplest things in life that I had previously just took for granted. My biggest accomplishment was that I learned how to go up four steps and then return down from those four steps. It was all a learning process. It took all of the energy that I could muster to do even the simplest of activities.

For some reason I started to get weaker and weaker. I had a harder time doing the activities that they planned for me. I started to run a fever and they just treated me with Tylenol. Dose after dose of Tylenol did nothing heroic for me. Within a period of time I went into a seizure. That episode readmitted me back into the regular part of the hospital. There they discovered that I now had an infection brewing in my bones by the incision site. I had a staphylococcus infection in my bones and if they didn't act quickly it could spread into my bloodstream and kill me. I was quickly taken back into surgery and a huge section of bone was removed from my head. After this surgery I could actually touch my brain right through my skin where they had removed that part of my skull.

This second and unexpected surgery took me back further. It took me miles and miles back to a land of difficulty, a land of struggling, a land I could never have even dreamed about. It was a nightmare that I never would have even imagined. I could no longer use the right side of my body. I had a stroke. It happened after the second surgery and it glared out at everybody.

My youngest son had the toughest time with it. He had trouble just looking at me. He saw me in the hospital bed and felt like there was no hope for his mother. No hope to see her walk again. No hope to see her pick up a cup with her right hand again. He saw my right arm and it did not even move an inch from under the sheets in the hospital bed. I fed myself with my left hand even though I am right handed. I needed to develop my left sided skills for I often spilled my drinks with my left hand. I simply was not used to using my left arm for skills that my right arm took care of. I often had crumbs of food fall down my clothes. It was hard for me to even see my food for I saw through the right eye while the left eye wore an eye shield.

After the second surgery I refused to go back to the rehabilitation part of the hospital for many reasons. One reason was that I felt like I had been in prison there and just wanted to go home. The second, more personal reason, was that I felt that I did not get good nursing care there. I got a mean infection in my incision that could have taken my life. I got a hospital acquired infection there under their roof. I kept those unhappy and untrusting thoughts to myself. I did not feel that I could come out and blame anyone so I kept those thoughts hidden. Due to my inner thoughts, I therefore demanded that I be discharged to my home. It caused a bit of confusion and the social service department was called into my case.

My son had to swear up and down and cross his heart that he would be home with me twenty-four/seven. They demanded that I never be left home alone. He agreed to all of their stipulations. He had to learn how to administer antibiotics and give me an anticoagulant, called Lovenox, subcutaneously into my abdomen. He had to learn how to administer my antibiotics through the vein through tubing called a PICC line. It was a tube that was threaded into a vein in my arm and went up to my chest. It would be there as my companion for the next six weeks and he had to be the caretaker of it. After he learned all the necessary medical treatment for his mother we headed home. I just wanted to go home. I hated each extra minute that I had to stay at the hospital.

I was wheeled out of the hospital up to the curb. Joel drove right up to the sidewalk to pick me up. With trepidation and his help, I clumsily and awkwardly climbed into the car. It was a novel experience, since I had not been in a car for many weeks. I slouched unevenly into the passenger side of the car and saw the world around me. I was happy to be leaving the walls of the hospital. My right eye surveyed all the cars, buildings and greenery around me. It was like the world didn't stop while I had temporarily stopped my living. Life was humming all around me as I watched with my one eye.

Time of Reflection

It was difficult for me to accept the fact that I could not take care of others. I could hardly take care of myself. I was not my old self. I used to be the one that handled all the problems within my family. I now was unable to even handle my own bills. I could not even hold a pen. I could not cook for myself or even clean my house. I could do very little. What happened next was a role reversal with my youngest son. He became the head of the household. I needed to accept that fact no matter how difficult it was for me to digest. He took on the role and did it well.

I was no longer the productive person I had been before the surgeries. In some ways I felt like I had lost myself and my identity. I felt that I lost my self worth. Through all of those struggles I still had to love myself and that was not an easy thing to do. I was able to do that by first loving my son Joel. I wanted to get better for him and in the process I started to love myself. I started to get better for myself.

There are situations in life that change the roles we get accustomed to. I was no longer the breadwinner or the head of the household. I had to quickly get used to my new roles. I had to accept the space I now occupied. Through all of it I had to still love myself. I had to accept who I was at the present moment. It wasn't an easy task to do but I had to do it. It came slowly one baby step at a time.

I soon became happy with the tiniest accomplishments. If I could pick up a penny with my right hand that was a huge accomplishment to me. When I struggled to put on one of my son's large tee shirts that was an accomplishment to me. My slightest achievements helped my self esteem.

Some of my friends out there might have lost their jobs. That could cause changes in self esteem and self confidence. Their jobs no longer define who they are and they could suffer from a deflated ego. Family situations could change from things such as a divorce or a death in the family. Some might have been in a car accident and others might have had changes in their health. No matter what the changes are we still need to love ourselves. We need to take care of ourselves and treat ourselves with respect. We need to take that first step of faith. It does not matter where the first step comes from, just know that the first step is the largest step. After that first step things start to come easier and quicker. After I could clumsily pick up a penny with my right hand, the sky was the limit. The same goes out there for my friends…so reach for the stars.

Chapter XII

Coming Home

I was relieved to return to my own abode. It felt like eons ago that I had entered my own home. I was coming home a different person. A person that could hardly walk. A much less capable and able person. My home was the same. It was still sitting on the same piece of land it had been resting on for a half a century. The outside grass, bushes and trees looked the same. Inside the furniture was exactly the same. Sofas, lights, beds, dressers, kitchen table were all the same. The only thing different was me. I could have never even dreamed of how I would be coming back. I was glad that I could not have seen into the future before I had the surgery. I might not have even gone through with it, had I known the outcome. It would have scared me out of the procedure. If I saw into the future I would have seen a horror film that would have made me sick. It would have pulled my guts out.

I came into my house with the help of my son. I needed help to walk those few feet into the front door. My ability to ambulate was poor. I could hardly walk and dragged my right leg behind with each step . I would step forward with my left leg and my right leg would try and follow but it did an extremely poor job of it. I was given a walker and I needed to get a bit stronger before I could walk with it. It was a blessing that there were no steps to climb to get into the house or else my son would have had to carry me in. My bedroom was on the same floor as the living room and this floor also had a bathroom so I was set. After the second surgery and suffering a stroke I could no longer climb steps. I could not even do one step. I remembered that after the first surgery, I struggled doing the four steps in rehab but at least I was able to do them. After the second surgery and stroke, steps were just a dream. It was hard to believe that after my first surgery I was actually eating with my right arm and working on steps. It just seemed like a foggy dream. Had I been dreaming or was that a true reality? The unhappy answer was, that it all had been a reality.

Simple activities were impossible or extremely difficult to accomplish. For one thing, I could not hold a pen with my right hand and I am right handed. It wasn't until months later that I clutched a pen awkwardly to write some big messy letters. I would practice writing on a local newspaper and try to write the big bold headings on the page. It was an accomplishment when I could write the title of an article. It was tiring and took time to do. It was like I was relearning how to do everything in my life.

My son took the checkbook from me and he paid all of our bills. I not only lacked the physical ability to write, but I also wasn't mentally there to process writing a check. He paid the bills, balanced the checkbook and ran a tight ship for there was little money coming in. In a way he became the parent of the house, and I was the child. It was role reversal to an extreme.

Every activity was a huge hurdle for me to accomplish. Just taking a shower was a huge production. My son had to remove the sliding glass doors that lead into the shower because I did not have the ability to climb in. The sliding glass doors were just too tricky for me to maneuver in and out of the shower with so he put up plastic shower curtains instead. In the shower I had a shower chair, so that I could sit while I showered. My right leg didn't have the ability to keep me standing safely in the shower. My son would make sure that I got in and sat safely and then he helped clean my back. I still had some modesty in my soul, so I would wash the rest of my body. Now, I did a poor job of it but as least I did it independently. Getting dressed after a shower was also a huge chore. I wore my son's elastic waist shorts for they were big and more manageable for me to get on. I could not work with clothes that had zippers or buttons. On my upper body I wore big tee-shirts. Those were the only clothes I wore because they were the only ones I could struggle to put on. It was hard to get the right arm in a shirt due to the stroke. I had to twist and turn the material to get it over the right shoulder and then get the arm through. I must admit that due to the difficulty of dressing I did not wear any underwear or a bra. That was just the honest truth. I did not have the ability or dexterity to perform such tasks. What had been the simplest things to do prior to my surgery had became a huge sometimes insurmountable task to do now.

I lived on one floor of my house but this floor did not have a kitchen on it. Thankfully my son took care of this issue also. He had so many issues to deal with. Joel would bring food upstairs for me to eat, in the living room, where I would spend most of my time. At that time food lost all of its interest to me. I found it a huge chore just to eat the smallest quantity. I probably ate less than six hundred calories a day. I do not know why I went through this time of disliking all food. It could have been the fact that I was no longer on steroids and I therefore lost that hunger drive. The same drive that had put fifteen to twenty unattractive pounds on my body. Granted, I was thrilled to be off those steroids, that were making my bones thin and my gut fat, but my inner body had gotten used to them. Another reason could have been the fact that I was on an antibiotics every eight hours and that could have taken away my appetite. I never figured out that answer. It was something new to me but I just had to go along with it.

One example, of my disinterest in food, was when my son Joel had brought up a hamburger for me to eat. It sat alone on a plate with nothing else near it. It was just a piece of ground meat cooked in a shape of a circle. For some reason I could not eat it, so I took it off the plate and wrapped in tissues. I then threw it away in the trash can. I hid the fact that I did not eat it from my son, for I knew he would be mad at me for not eating. He was acting like the parent and parents do not like it when their kids don't eat their food and waste it. Shame on me.

My gastrointestinal tract, in other words my gut, also had troubling issues. I had to go number two, have a bowel movement, about ten times a day. I remember once going sixteen times in one day. Why did I have this problem, I didn't have colitis or any known intestinal problem? What caused that trouble when I had operations way up in my head not in my gut? I now believe it was from those nasty strong antibiotics I had to take every eight hours. My son gave me my antibiotic every eight hours around the clock through the line called a PICC line. I think it was the antibiotics that wreaked havoc with my gut. It killed bacteria of any sort even those that helped my body. I believed the antibiotics did not get along with my intestinal bacteria and caused an inner war of their own. I usually felt sick and nauseated until the afternoon hours. I felt nauseous in the morning hours and spent my time visiting the bathroom. Mornings became a dreadful time of the day.

Was there any fun or enjoyable moments in my days? With all this free time on my hands one would think that I was having a blast. No more rushing to work, paying the bills, visiting my parents, or helping my children. In reality there was no fun to be had. I did not even enjoy watching T.V. I lacked the mental ability to stay concentrated on a show or a story.

I still also carried the problem of trying to see the world through just one eye. The left eye could not be free to explore and look around the world it lived in. It was kept behind a black shutter. I wore an eye patch over my left eye so that I could see the world as one. It seemed like the left eye felt jealous of the fact that I did not let it see the world. It only saw darkness, a part of my world, a part that truly did exist. I figured that with an eye patch over my left eye I looked like a pirate. I am sure that many people thought I looked kind of strange. They would quickly look in a different direction so that they did not appear like they were staring at me.

Despite the inability to dress appropriately, and the feelings of weakness and nausea, I did have moments of trying to move forward. I had a physical and an occupational therapist come to my home once a week. They were the highlights of my week. I had to be up and ready for when they arrived. The occupational therapist was a pusher in a good sense. He wanted me to accomplish more than I could but that was his helpful inward drive. I remember trying to pick up pennies with my right hand. I had to move the pennies from the left side of my body to the right side. With extreme concentration and effort I would take my quivery, weak, uncoordinated right arm and reach for one penny and transport it a few feet away. It was not an easy task and took much effort to accomplish, for my fingers did not even have the dexterity to grab a penny. It took a massive amount of effort and skill. I also had to practice bringing an empty cup to my mouth. I got scared when the therapist put an ounce of water in the cup. I got close to spilling the water many times. By the time the therapist was done working with me I was washed out. He used his time with me wisely and never let a minute go by without some effort on my part.

My biggest accomplishment, with the physical therapist, was trying to go down a few steps that led into my back yard. I was completely scared by the mere thought of doing it. Something that took no effort before in my life seemed like a huge undertaking. The physical therapist and my son where right there next to me when I first tried this enormous activity. They both supported some of my weight as I tried this new skill. My left leg would go and do the primary work and my other leg would meekly follow. I had to relearn skills that once were so easy to do.

Walking soon became a large focus of my days. I first started walking the distance in front of my house, which was about 24 feet wide. That was my first accomplishment. I would walk the width of my house a few times with the walker and then tiredly sit on a chair on the porch to recover from the effort. I eventually went out on to the street with my son and the walker. I did not care how I looked for vanity was not tolerated. I was out there to get better. I wore my eye patch and my son's shorts and tee shirts to trek the first block of my neighborhood. Eventually I got the courage to walk the block with the walker by myself. My left leg would lead the trip and my right leg limped behind. It was a very slow pace but I was moving forward.

After six weeks I was finally finished with the antibiotics. I was done having those bacteria killers live in my veins. The PICC line was about to be removed and I was rejoicing. Since I no longer needed someone to give me my antibiotics I felt freer. At that time I decided to go and live with my mother for a short while. My son had put in a lot of time and effort into me and needed a well deserved break.

I was driven down to my mother's house by Joel. I settled into my mother's house and started a regimen of walking. I had used the walker for the last six weeks and just wanted to be finished with it. I had been told by my physical therapist that I would need my walker for a bit longer and then I should gradually use a cane when I walked. On my own stubbornness, I ditched the walker and just let it sit collecting dust in the corner. I also let the thought of a cane go out the window. I started my limping outside my mother's house without any helping hands or tools. I walked with just my wobbly legs and the air around me. I walked and I walked and I even walked some more. It was a positive event and I was going to keep going with it. I didn't work, I didn't cook, I didn't drive a vehicle, and I didn't do housework, but I did walk and that was my accomplishment.

It seemed that once I had one problem resolved I would then concentrate heavily on another problem. Walking had improved and I was now going up and down the steps slowly holding on to the banister. Since that problem was slowly resolving my eye problem took my attention. My eye patch continued to be a problem and I still had the double vision. My mother took me to an eye doctor and the doctor ran tests on me. She felt that I could end up with double vision for the rest of my life. I did not like that conclusion one bit. She did give me some eye exercises to do and said she would see me in a few weeks.

I was instructed to exercise my eyes for a total of five minutes every four hours. I was told to remove the eye patch for that brief period of time and to concentrate on items around me. I practiced much more than instructed and I did it every hour with stubborn determination. Again it was my stubbornness that kept that strong push in my soul. In my mother's kitchen I started with my first eye exercises. I taped up a piece of paper that had the numbers twelve, three, six, and nine on it like the numbers on a clock. I would concentrate on one number at a time and try to see it as one. Once in a while this would work for a second. I would see the number twelve as one not my normal two.

I decided that I needed more help with this task than I could do alone. I needed help from the powers above. Who else could I plead to for help but to the powers above? I started to light a candle every night at the same time and pray. My mother would pray with me. I asked for single vision, and here is when things got interesting.

From the powers above along with my own stubbornness, I started to have one to two minute periods of seeing things as single. This took all of my concentration and effort. I would not stop the exercises and the healing would not stop either.

During this time my mother often took me with her to see a classical concert. She often went to these concerts with her friends. I would just sit there concentrating on a person playing an instrument. I was amazed that for a few moments I saw the person with the instrument as one. When I went back to the eye doctor's office a few weeks later she retested my eyes. The doctor was initially speechless. Something quite extraordinary had happened. Something unspeakable had happened. Something unexplainable happened. I was able to take the eye test with both eyes open and see single. I needed to hold my head at a very specific angle but it worked. As long as I looked forward in that one angle I was able to make my world of two become a world of one. The slightest downward shift of my eyes turned my world into two again, but at my special angle I saw things as one. I could see single in a certain magical way and that was a huge blessing. I remembered tears just flowing down my face when I was in the eye doctor's office. I could not stop the tears as my mother handled the payments at the registration desk. I cried in the waiting room where other people were sitting. I could not stop the tears of joy. I am crying now as I write this to share with you. So even if you don't believe or have moments of doubt, know that there is something very special out there. A power from above and a power from within. A power that loves you.

My mother felt her work was done and it was time for me to return to my home base. My son came the next day to pick me up and take me home. I now could be left home alone. I remember the first time my son left me home alone for an hour. I was more scared than a kid. I just stayed on the couch afraid to doing anything. What if something would happen and I was all alone? It was all so frightening to me. It took time for me to regain the confidence of being home alone.

My next big step was driving a car, my Honda Civic which was a stick shift. I needed to relearn how to operate one of my good old friends, my Honda. My son took me into an almost vacant parking lot to see if I was able to drive. The stick shift had three pedals on the floor. My son asked me what the pedals were for. Well, of course, I knew which one was the gas pedal but I had trouble verbally figuring out the other two. I was able to figure it out by letting my feet do the talking. I put her into first gear but stalled out a few times. By the end of my ten minute practice I was able to go from first to third gear and back down again. My son, who was the parent at this time, watched what I did ever so carefully. He then drove us home.

The funny thing about this whole ordeal was that I taught my son how to drive a stick shift a few years back. I taught my son how to drive that car. I was now the one being taught. I have some very fond memories of teaching him how to drive. He actually got the car into third gear when he was only eleven years old. Back then we were also in a near by vacant parking lot. Little did we know that the roles would be reversed years later. After a few more times with my son Joel, I tried driving by myself. I took myself to a shopping center that was close by. The store was just four miles away but it seemed like a huge journey. Since I felt like an inexperienced driver it was a huge journey for me, but I made it.

Time of Reflection

To this day I am still grateful that I was given single vision when I look straight. Do miracles really happen? Well since it happened to me I now believe that they do. Miracles come in all shapes and sizes and often come when least expected. The truth is I believe it could happen to all of my friends out there. Just have the faith and unexplainable things can happen. I hope that all of you get the help your soul desires.

Chapter XIII

Getting a New Grip on Life

After the surgery I had to relearn everything. I needed to relearn how to bring a cup of juice to my mouth with my right hand. I had to relearn how to walk. I had to relearn how to dress myself. I had to relearn how to write. I had to relearn how to remember simple things like a conversation. It was all very hard. Another thing that was hard was to accept the fact that I could no longer help others. I could hardly help myself. I had to depend on my son to write the bills, prepare my meals, do the laundry, and clean the house.

Prior to the surgery it was my desire and my nature to help others. Now that was not possible. My son had to be my parent. He had to be my caretaker. He had to be the one to watch over me. My son had to now take out school loans for college, and that made me feel like a failure. I was no longer able to be the financial helper that

I used to be. I needed to refigure things out from the beginning. Mentally and physically I had to start from the raw beginning.

At the beginning of my recovery, I lost the ability to hold back any idea or thought processes that was in my head. I was liberal in my conversations. I was not careful and reserved with conversation like I had been prior in my life. They do say that people that have had brain surgeries go through this period in their lives. Their brains no longer control what comes out of their mouth. Normally we are all conditioned to watch and weigh what words actually come out of our mouths. Thoughts could go through wildly but speech has to be modified and humbled.

I also had another common symptom, I cried frequently. I cried at the drop of a hat over anything. I often cried daily. It was part of my daily routine. Tissues and I became inseparably close friends. My son would instruct me not to cry when we were out in public. Once when we were signing in at the doctor's office he told me not to cry. Just the thought of it made me cry. He could do nothing to make the tears have limited spaces and times. He never had a mother that cried so much, but I was still his mother.

After all my medical trials and tribulations there was a time of re-examining life. I met many different people on my path and made friends with people in the neighborhood that I never knew before. It was during this time that different perspectives came into my life.

I met one person that was a retired truck driver. I would talk to him every time I saw him on my walks. I would just tell him my life story as if I had known him for years. Often I would cry but that didn't seem to matter to him for he would still listened attentively. Though we were different in many ways we shared those moments as if we had been buddies for a long time. I soon learned that he had see most of the United States during his truck travels. He had also seen the inside of a prison cell, a sight I had never seen. I shared and talked to him and he shared and talked to me. Through our discussions I started to see life in a different way.

He did not understand why I had never stood up for myself. He did not understand why I was always giving to my kids. He felt that I had taken on too much heavy responsibility with money. He did not understand why I took abuse from my ex-husbands. He even wondered why I would have even married such men. I slowly learned that maybe I had been doing some things wrong. Maybe I had to think of myself first. That was something I had forgotten how to do. I needed to think about myself first. I needed to love myself first.

It was through my new friends, that I started to learn that I did not have to give endlessly to gain affection. I needed to stop being so generous to the point of hurting myself. One major change was that I needed to let my daughter figure out her own life. I did not have to pick up her bills. Even though I worried about my grandchildren, I had to worry about my own bills, first.

Alice did not enjoy her new mother that was emerging. She was actually mad that the money stopped coming from me and she did say some unkind things to me. I had to hold on tight to my new way of thinking or else I would be back to where I had started from. I needed to stay straight and not give in to my old self. I could no longer cave in and give and give. I believed that in time she would change, and I was willing to wait. I needed to let her do it on her own, and I needed to learn how to save money for myself.

After the brain tumor it became harder to save money for I was no longer able to function as a registered nurse. I felt inept and nervous about doing things that I used to do with my eyes closed. The job situation did have me in moments of complete anxiety. I would cry the night before I had to go to work and get an ill stomach a few miles before I reached my destination. My friends helped me through this difficult situation. I needed to change my job in order to live a normal life, a life that was not filled with anxiety and dread. I am not sure why I could no longer work doing what I used to do, but it was a reality and I had to accept it. I had to love myself for the way I was. I had to love myself for being a different person. I had to accept the road I was traveling on. This brings me to the reason I wrote this book. I learned one important lesson. It took me forty-nine years to learn it but I have now figured it out. We have to love ourselves first.

As your friend here on this earth I ask you to love yourself first. We need to take care of ourselves first before we can take care of others. I know it is a special thing to take care of others, but we have to make ourselves our first priority. If I had loved myself first I might not have married my first husband. I might have saved my own money that I worked hard for on myself. I might not have had a brain tumor for maybe I would have had a less stressful life. I might have felt more confident in myself if I had loved myself first. I might have had a better feeling about myself if I did not let others take advantage of me. We need to start now and treat ourselves better. I know that many of you out there skimp on yourselves, but please love yourself first. You are worth it!

As children, some of us might not have had a positive influence, but as teenagers and adults we have the power to conquer any bad feelings that were engrained in us. Maybe your mother or your father called you names. Maybe the person that raised you pushed you around to the point of abuse. Maybe your brother or sister was treated better than you and they were put up on a pedestal. Maybe your present life with a husband or wife is making you feel like a fraction of a person. Maybe a boss is treating you poorly and that is effecting your self-esteem. Maybe coming from a divorced family you have feelings of worthlessness about yourself. Maybe being overweight makes you feel bad about yourself. It could be a number of reason, too many reasons to count. It could come from being homosexual to having a physical deformity such as a limp or distorted physical features. Well, the truth is I think you are great and the power within me loves you. That power lies within all of us and we have the power to conquer those bad feelings.

Yes, it could take time, because many of us have years to unravel. The unraveling process might need coaching from a psychologist, or maybe help from a close friend. The first step is to recognize the problem and then decide to take yourself seriously. You deserve to be treated kindly. No longer allow yourself to be treated like a second class person. That was the past, now is the present and it is time to love yourself first. Those negative feeling need to be turned around and made into positive feelings. We all need to have positive feelings inside and out. Now is the time to stop feeling bad. Now is the time to love yourself. Anyone can love themselves first. A teenager can, a young adult can, a middle aged person can, and a senior citizen can. You have the power to do it, so love yourself first.

After having three difficult surgeries to my head I needed to reexamine my life. I had to reassess its meaning and why I even stayed alive. Many questions came to me at different times throughout my recovery. I somehow knew that many of my questions would go unanswered, but not all of them. One specific question had a very strong answer, an answer that was so simple. I had to learn to love myself first. Loving myself came first. I pray that all of my friend out there, where ever they might be, please *love yourselves first.*

This autobiography takes us through the joys and sorrows of someone's life. In this book we can see how the lowest moments can build up into the highest moments. We will get an open glimpse into the trek the author took. She openly shares her private journey as she moves forward. When she gets the diagnosis of a brain tumor her whole life changes. Through her personal journey she shares her inner thoughts and questions. The questions ultimately take us into the core of her soul. Through her difficulties she learns a very valuable lesson. This takes us to the reason the book was written. CAT wants you to see how important it is to love oneself first.

CAT had always been someone that enjoyed helping others. She enjoyed being a mother and worked tirelessly as a registered nurse. It gave her a productive and meaningful life. Things seemed to be going along smoothly at the surface, but underneath things were bumpy. Some of the bumps turned into tow divorces. Through all of those heart aches she continued to push forward, strangely enough there was something that she could never push past. She was not even sure what the hurdle was that she needed to tackle. It wasn't until after CAT was diagnosed with a brain tumor that a certain problem would quietly resurface. After going trough three tricky surgeries and suffering a stroke something came into her vision. She realized that she needed to love herself fist, that one huge but simple revelation opened up her eyes. It brought her to writing this book for all to see.